SNAP SHOT™

Art director Roger Priddy
Editor Mary Ling
Designers David Gillingwater,
Sharon Grant

Photography by
Frank Greenaway, Neil Fletcher,
Jane Burton, Kim Taylor,
Stephen Oliver and Colin Keates

A Dorling Kindersley book

First published in Great Britain in 1994
by Snapshot™,
an imprint of Covent Garden Books
9 Henrietta Street, London, WC2E 8PS

Second printing 1994

Copyright © 1994 Covent Garden
Books Limited,
London

ISBN 1-85948-015-2
Colour reproduction by Colourscan
Printed in Belgium by Proost

INCREDIBLE MINI-BEASTS

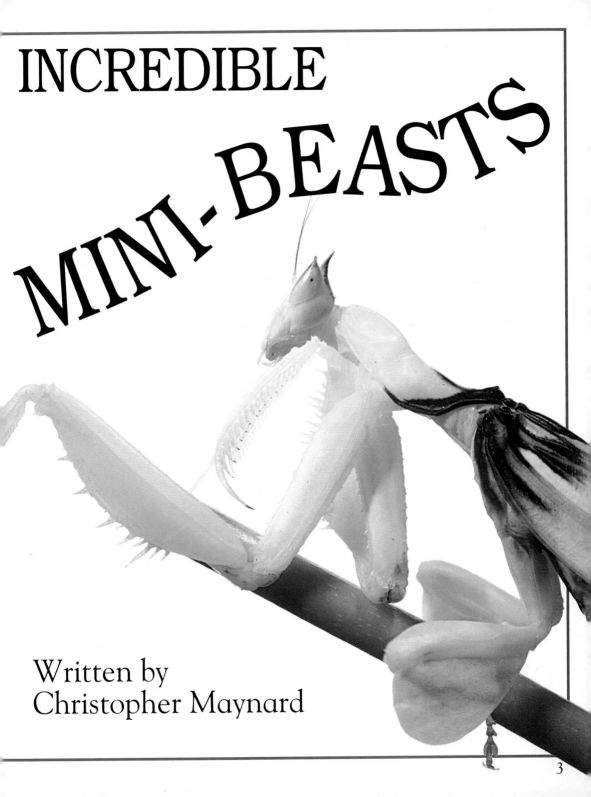

Written by
Christopher Maynard

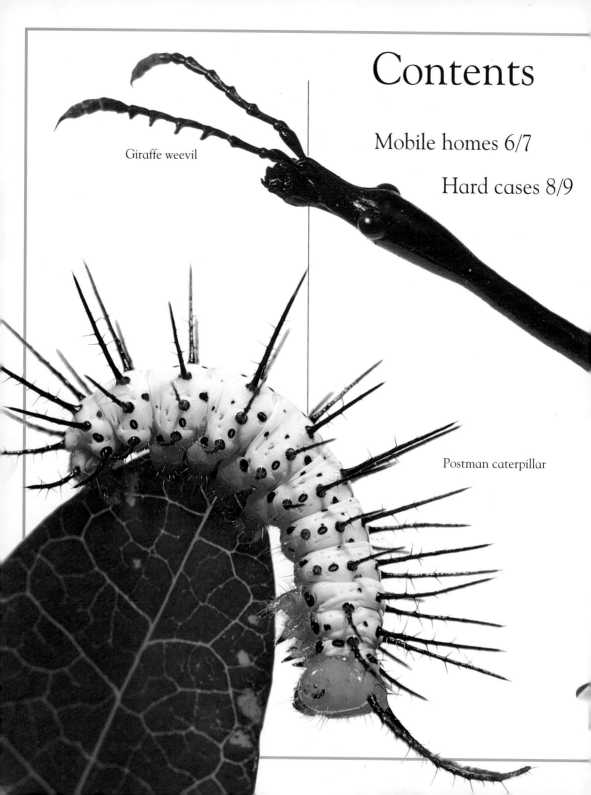

Contents

Giraffe weevil

Postman caterpillar

Mobile homes

Some animals are happy with just one fixed address. Others have homes that are small enough to move anywhere they choose.

The home that grows

Shell thickens and grows stronger

Hermit crab

Great pond snail

Home extension
The great pond snail has a long, twisted shell on its back. As it grows, it builds a bigger shell. Only its head and foot peek out.

Adult caddis flies look a lot like moths

Stuck at home
A caddis fly larva spins a tube of silk around its body. It sticks sand, pebbles, and bits of plants over this to hide itself.

Caddis fly larva

Wherever it goes ... home goes, too!

Caddis larvae use glue and silk to make cases

Trading places
A hermit crab lives in borrowed shells. When it outgrows one shell, it moves to a new and bigger one - like this empty whelk shell.

Hard cases

There are more kinds of beetles than any other animal in the world. We know about 300,000 species so far, compared to only 4,500 types of mammals.

Tiny giraffe
The giraffe weevil is a kind of beetle with a very long neck. Nobody knows why it is this shape.

Ladybird

A neck twice as long as its body

Giraffe weevil

Beetles and weevils have tough wing cases that shield most of their body

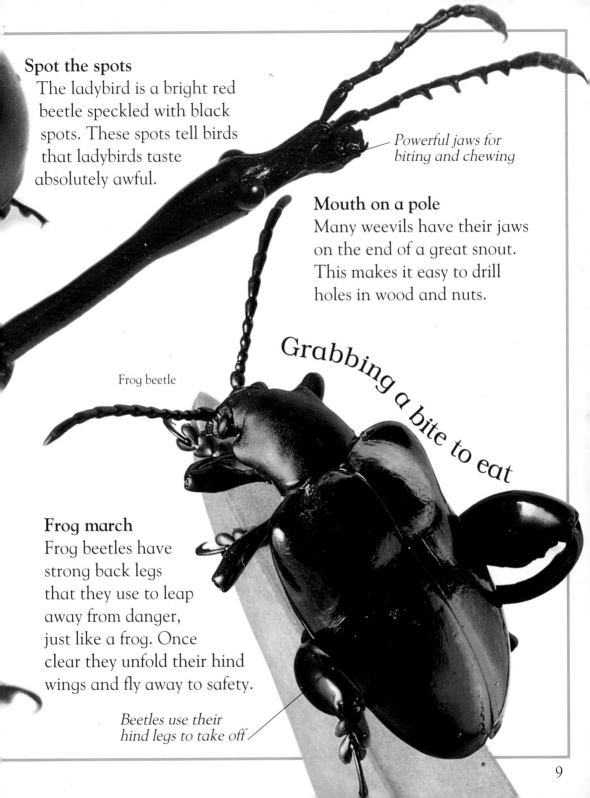

Spot the spots

The ladybird is a bright red beetle speckled with black spots. These spots tell birds that ladybirds taste absolutely awful.

Powerful jaws for biting and chewing

Mouth on a pole

Many weevils have their jaws on the end of a great snout. This makes it easy to drill holes in wood and nuts.

Frog beetle

Grabbing a bite to eat

Frog march

Frog beetles have strong back legs that they use to leap away from danger, just like a frog. Once clear they unfold their hind wings and fly away to safety.

Beetles use their hind legs to take off

Munching machines

Caterpillars are little eating machines.
A single one can polish off all the leaves
on a bush during a few days of
non-stop feasting.

They like spike!
This postman caterpillar has sharp,
poisonous spikes, all along its back to
protect it from hungry birds.

Gobbles thousand

Long spikes

Postman
caterpillar

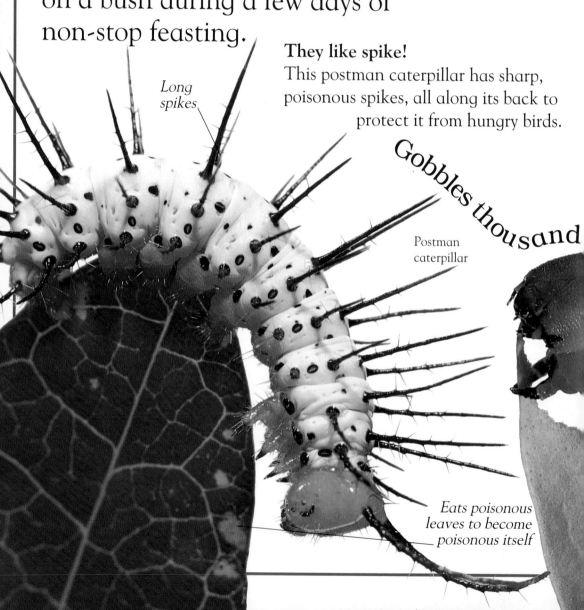

*Eats poisonous
leaves to become
poisonous itself*

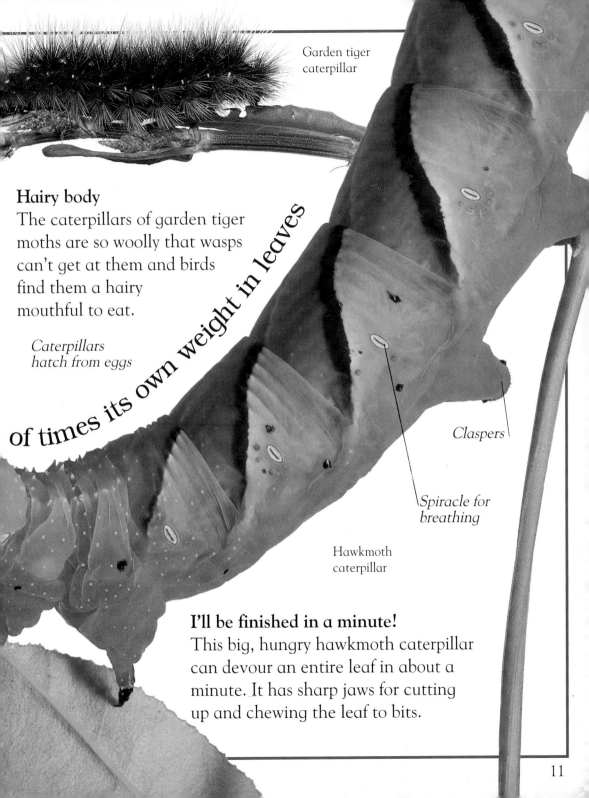

Garden tiger caterpillar

Hairy body

The caterpillars of garden tiger moths are so woolly that wasps can't get at them and birds find them a hairy mouthful to eat.

Caterpillars hatch from eggs

of times its own weight in leaves

Claspers

Spiracle for breathing

Hawkmoth caterpillar

I'll be finished in a minute!

This big, hungry hawkmoth caterpillar can devour an entire leaf in about a minute. It has sharp jaws for cutting up and chewing the leaf to bits.

Butterflies and moths

Most butterflies are busy during the day while moths mainly fly around at night. Aside from that, moths are often a drab brown, while butterflies have glorious coloured wings.

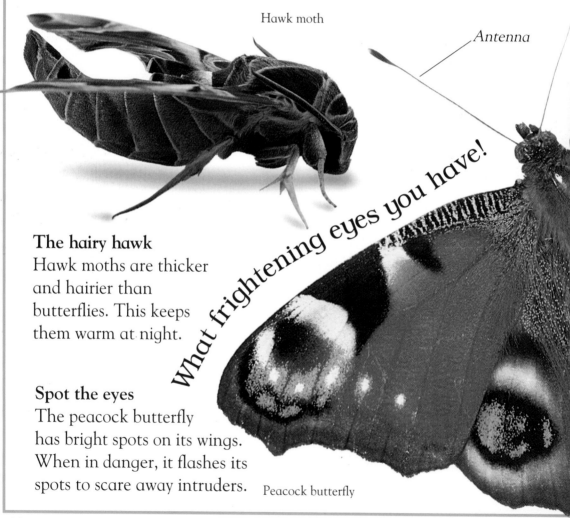

Hawk moth

Antenna

The hairy hawk
Hawk moths are thicker and hairier than butterflies. This keeps them warm at night.

What frightening eyes you have!

Spot the eyes
The peacock butterfly has bright spots on its wings. When in danger, it flashes its spots to scare away intruders.

Peacock butterfly

A lady's scent
Male moths can smell females with their antennae.

Sipping nectar
The bush moth has a long tube tongue for dipping deep into flowers and sucking up nectar.

What is making that smell?

Wing patterns are made up of thousands of tiny scales

These pretty spots are not for decoration

Bush moth

A butterfly sucks nectar through its straw-shaped 'proboscis'

Seriously deadly

A hairy tarantula may be scary to look at, but watch out for its bite! It is deadly to birds and small animals, but only as bad as a bee sting to human beings.

Look out for a spider that's big and hairy!

Tarantula

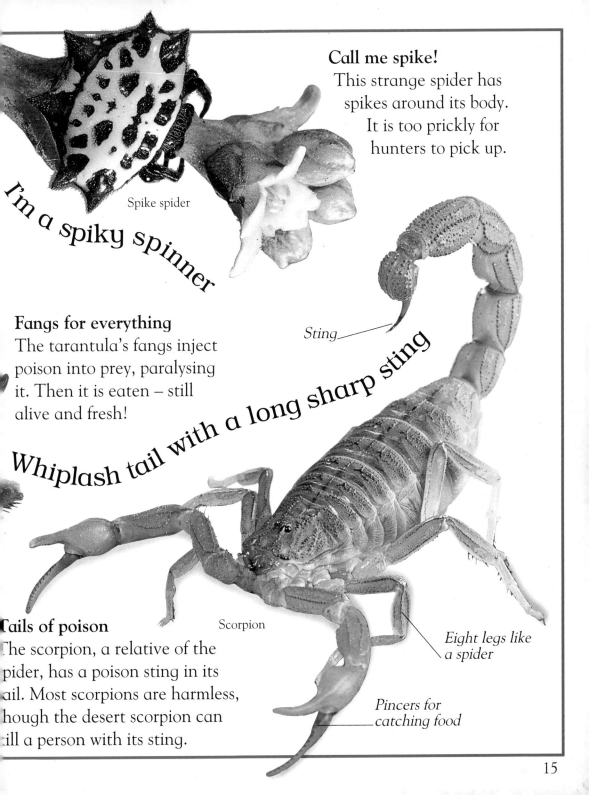

Call me spike!
This strange spider has spikes around its body. It is too prickly for hunters to pick up.

Spike spider

I'm a spiky spinner

Fangs for everything
The tarantula's fangs inject poison into prey, paralysing it. Then it is eaten – still alive and fresh!

Sting

Whiplash tail with a long sharp sting

Tails of poison
The scorpion, a relative of the spider, has a poison sting in its tail. Most scorpions are harmless, though the desert scorpion can kill a person with its sting.

Scorpion

Eight legs like a spider

Pincers for catching food

15

Damsels and dragons

Most dragonflies are bigger than damselflies, though they look much the same. At rest, they hold their wings outspread. Damselflies fold their wing up over their bodies.

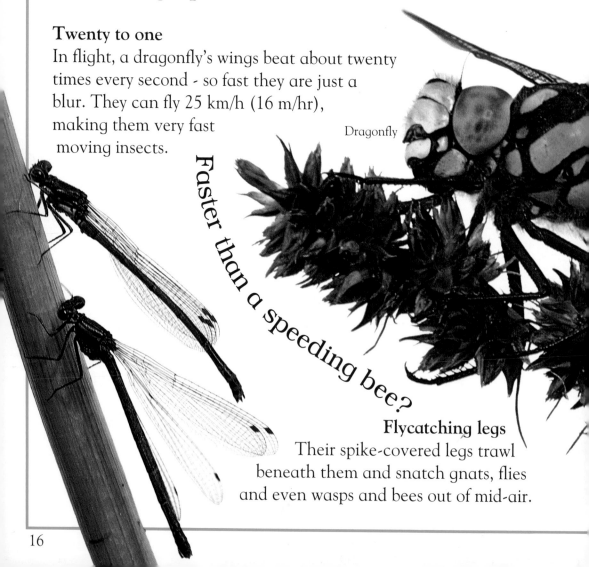

Twenty to one
In flight, a dragonfly's wings beat about twenty times every second - so fast they are just a blur. They can fly 25 km/h (16 m/hr), making them very fast moving insects.

Dragonfly

Faster than a speeding bee?

Flycatching legs
Their spike-covered legs trawl beneath them and snatch gnats, flies and even wasps and bees out of mid-air.

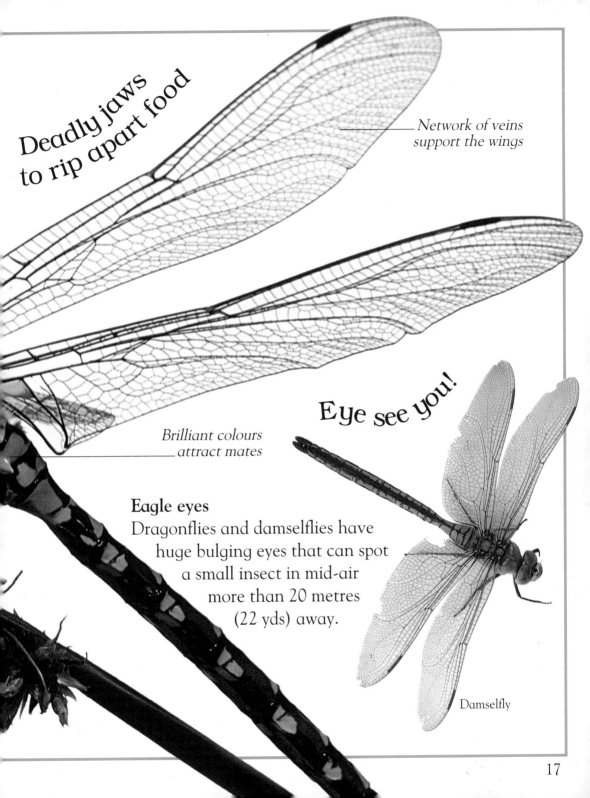

Deadly jaws to rip apart food

Network of veins support the wings

Brilliant colours attract mates

Eye see you!

Eagle eyes
Dragonflies and damselflies have huge bulging eyes that can spot a small insect in mid-air more than 20 metres (22 yds) away.

Damselfly

Lots of legs!

Most people think a millipede has 1,000 legs, while a centipede has 100. But millipedes only have up to 750 legs, while centipedes have from 30 to 354.

Long legged and built for speed

Millipede

Legs move in waves – so they don't get tangled

Nibble, nibble
Millipedes graze on algae or nibble on plan Some are even garden pests. They come out at night to feed. By day, they hide in dark places.

Centipedes have much longer legs than millipedes

Seven times more
Compared to humans, most insects have an incredible number of legs. The common woodlouse, for example, has 14 legs in all.

Woodlouse

Antenna

Death by poison
Centipedes hunt snails, worms and insects, injecting poison into prey with their terrible fangs.

Beware the poison fang!

Giant tiger centipede

The sting thing

Bees and wasps have a needle-sharp sting at the end of their tails. It delivers venom that really hurts. Bees can only sting once, then they die. Wasps can sting many times.

Beware of the sting in the tail!

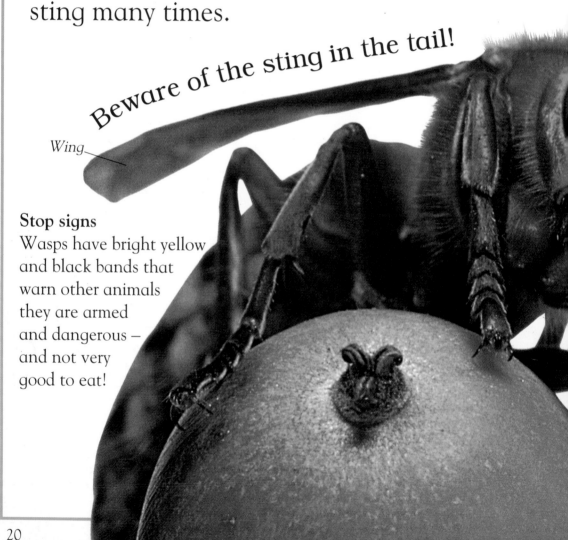

Wing

Stop signs
Wasps have bright yellow and black bands that warn other animals they are armed and dangerous – and not very good to eat!

The honey bunch
When honey bees land on a
flower they suck up the sweet
nectar with their tube-shaped
mouths. Back at the hive, the
nectar is turned into honey.

Bee

Bulging eyes

Wasp

The easy way of making honey

Recycled paper
Wasp nests are built
from wood fibre that
has been chewed up
to make paper. A
single egg is laid in
each six-sided cell.

*Powerful jaws
are used for
digging and
cutting up food*

*Growing
larva*

Bug eat bug

Insects that live by killing other insects need to be fast and strong. One of the best known hunters is the praying mantis.

Praying mantis

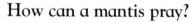

When is a leaf a stick?

The giant spiny stick-insect looks like an old withered leaf as it sits on a branch. It blends in with leaves so well that few hunters ever spot it.

Front legs

Giant stick insect

How can a mantis pray?

The praying mantis gets its name from the way it sits at rest, quietly waiting for an insect to draw near. It keeps its legs folded up before its face, as if it is saying its prayers.

Just praying to be picked?

Orchid mantis

The leaf bites back!

Flower power
The deadly orchid
mantis hides among
orchids, pretending
to be a flower.

*Green body
helps to hide it
among leaves*

Handy legs

Grasshoppers and crickets have long hind legs and strong thigh muscles that are handy for taking terrific leaps and bounds.

King of the spring!
A cricket folds its long legs back, then springs upwards.

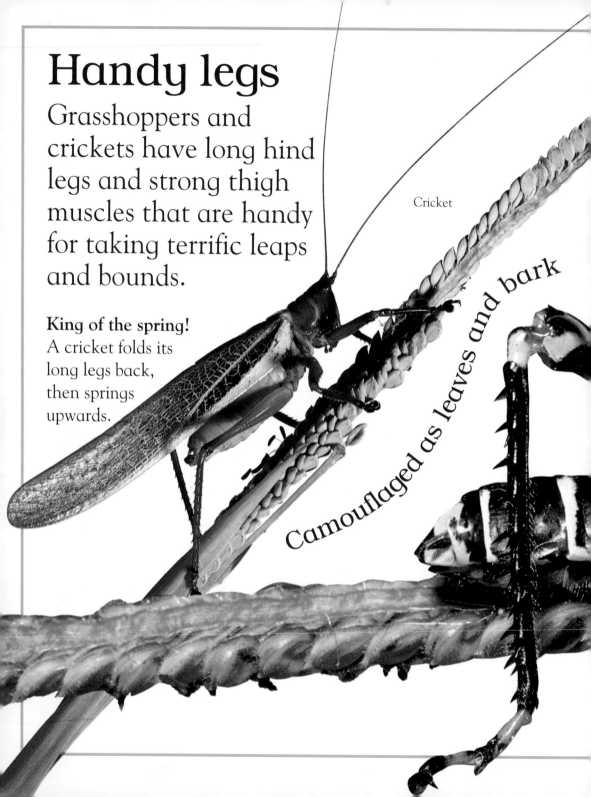

Cricket

Camouflaged as leaves and bark

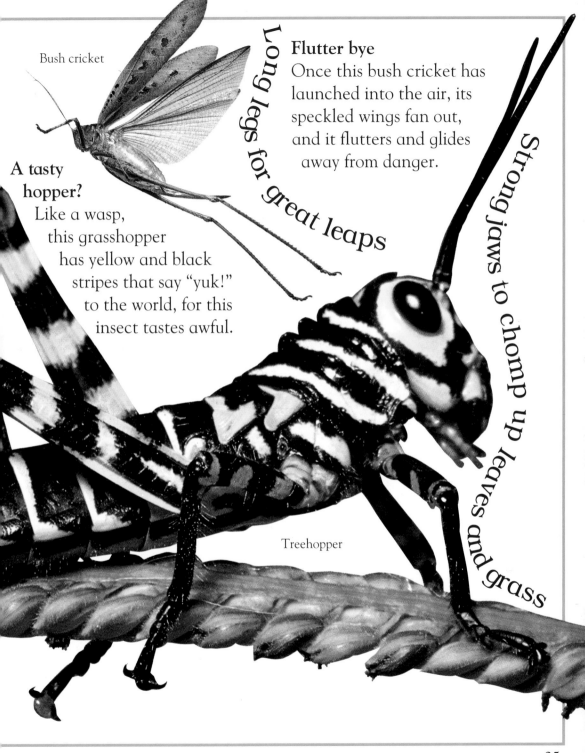

Bush cricket

Long legs for great leaps

Flutter bye
Once this bush cricket has
launched into the air, its
speckled wings fan out,
and it flutters and glides
away from danger.

**A tasty
hopper?**
Like a wasp,
this grasshopper
has yellow and black
stripes that say "yuk!"
to the world, for this
insect tastes awful.

Strong jaws to chomp up leaves and grass

Treehopper

Old folks at home

Cockroaches have made their home on Earth for over 320 million years, long enough to watch the dinosaurs roam the land and then disappear. During this time, they have hardly changed at all.

Antennae help find the way in the dark

Cockroach

Home on the range
Cockroaches live almost anywhere. Several kinds have moved into human homes, where kitchens full of food crumbs are their favourite place.

Who's feasting under the fridge?

Dark and damp

Some cockroaches love to live in caves, where it is dark and damp. Here they feed on almost anything: plants, fungi, dead animals, droppings.

The flat body allows the cockroach to scurry into tiny crevices

Young thing

Adults have a hard, shiny case to protect their wings. This cockroach is still too young to have grown any wings.

Young cockroach

Many mouths to feed

Insects feed in many ways. Some have strong jaws for tearing food to bits before they chew it up. Others have mouths best suited for piercing and sucking.

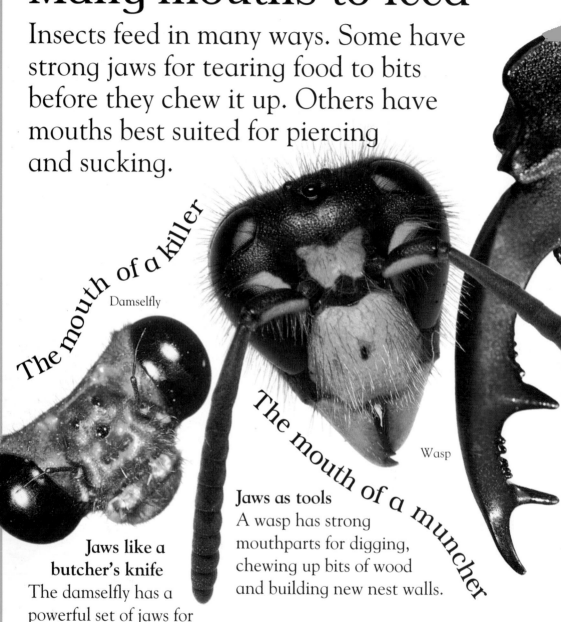

The mouth of a killer

Damselfly

The mouth of a muncher

Wasp

Jaws like a butcher's knife
The damselfly has a powerful set of jaws for tearing its prey apart live.

Jaws as tools
A wasp has strong mouthparts for digging, chewing up bits of wood and building new nest walls.

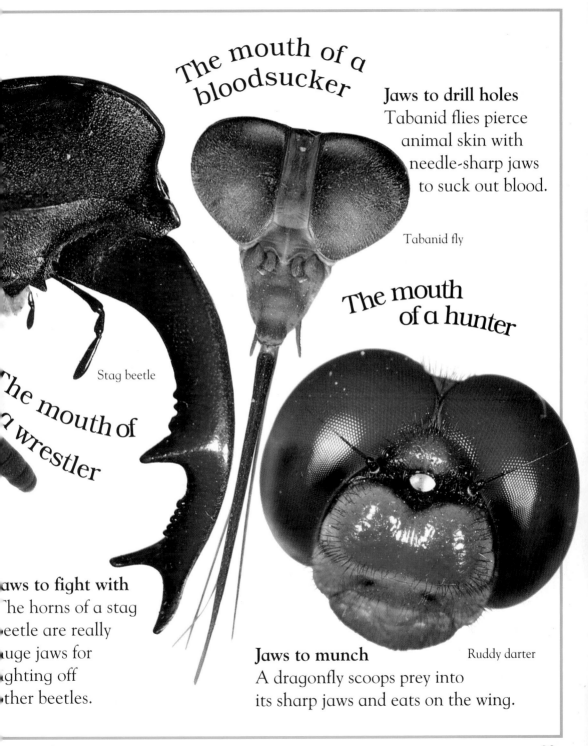

The mouth of a bloodsucker

Jaws to drill holes
Tabanid flies pierce animal skin with needle-sharp jaws to suck out blood.

Tabanid fly

Stag beetle

The mouth of a wrestler

Jaws to fight with
The horns of a stag beetle are really huge jaws for fighting off other beetles.

The mouth of a hunter

Jaws to munch Ruddy darter
A dragonfly scoops prey into its sharp jaws and eats on the wing.

Index

Five fiendish questions

1. Which insect dresse[...] up in pebbles and san[...]

2. How long does it take a caterpillar to eat a leaf?

(a) about 1 second
(b) about 1 minute
(c) about 1 hour
(d) several days
(e) caterpillars don't eat leaves

3. Which sense does a male moth use to find a female?

(a) sight (b) sound
(c) smell (d) taste
(e) touch

4. Will you die if a tarantula bites you?

5. How does a dragonf[...] catch its prey?

Answers on page 32

Are ladybirds always red with

black spots?

Answer on next page

Answers

From page 30 :   1. The caddis fly larva.
                              2. About one minute.
                              3. Smell
                              4. No, but the bite is as
                                     painful as a bee sting.
                              5. With its legs.

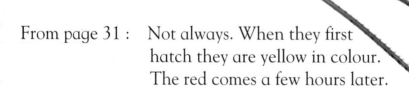

From page 31 :   Not always. When they first
hatch they are yellow in colour.
The red comes a few hours later.